Peace & harmony

Stefka Harp

Peace & harmony
© Stefka Mladenova 2020

All rights reserved. No part of this publication may be reproduced, stored in a retrieval system, or transmitted in any form or by any means, electronic, mechanical, photocopying, recording or otherwise, without the prior written permission of the author.

National Library of Australia Cataloguing Statement:

A catalogue record for this book is available from the National Library of Australia

ISBN: 9780648405580

Published with the assistance of www.wordwrightediting.com.au

Images courtesy of clker.com and bigstockphotos.com.

www.stefkaharp.com

Peace & harmony

Contents

Acknowledgements v

Dedication vi

Introduction vii

Peace 1

Serenity 2

Divine love 3

Love, peace and harmony 4

To be holy is the key for peace and harmony 6

My harmonious thoughts are pure heart 8

My good deeds are my needs 10

On the Divine I can count for eternal peace to find ... 12

I am an image of the Holy 14

Devotion to the Holy 16

Blessed I am salvation to find 18

Serenity in all its might 20

Patience creates peace within 22

I cherish the peace within 24

Blessings for all 26

My days of joy 27

Peace brings life to fruition 28

Peace within brings wisdom 30

I wish and command 32

Harmony bestowed 34

I am here now, the Almighty whispered 36

Young and vibrant we are 38

Divine blessings 40

Body and soul 41

Glorified 42

Harmonious I am 43

Arts in society 44

Serenity within 46

Gail Cartwright, Editor 48

Harmony 50

About the author 51

Peace & harmony

Acknowledgements

I wish to express my deep and sincere gratitude to my parents for teaching me the value of life — how to love and be happy as well as show kindness — and my siblings, for being a part of my life.

My thanks go to the Australian Government for opening the door for me to migrate and become a permanent resident; to experience a different kind of life, culture and customs, which have been very enriching, enlightening and eye-opening. I'm very grateful for the opportunity I've been given to get to the point I'm at.

Sincere gratitude to:

- my daughter Boyana for her patience and loving assistance in proofreading my work, as well as Jean White from Moorooka
- Gail, publishing advisor for the guidance given.

Stefka Harp

Dedication

Everything I write and have written so far is dedicated to the Almighty who has guided me through life without me being aware. At times, my ignorance and oblivion to the facts revealed have led to strife and suffering. But these experiences have given me the much-needed fuel for my writings, and I hope they will help others. Life is like a jigsaw puzzle. Some things are meant to happen so that the pieces fit within the puzzle and we come to know the truth. Also gratitude to my parents for bringing me into this world and giving me much needed love and care, as well as gratitude to the rest of the family for being part of my life.

S.H.

Disclaimer: The author is expressing beliefs and views based on her life experience. There is no intention to offend anyone who has contrary views. The poems are fun to read and in the process can bring a positive and loving attitude.

Introduction

Peace and harmony is my last set of poems in this series of eight books. Each of them captures one important feeling of many that each of us have, therefore releasing thought energies continuously.

1. *Heart and soul* is all about thoughts, feelings and deeds. Thoughts spark feelings and feelings create more thoughts, and it goes back and forth.

2. *Love Divine* is all to do with universal love. By repeating these words, powerful thought energy is created to take you through life's ups and downs.

3. *Forgiveness and beyond*, as the title suggests, is all about forgiveness, a powerful emotional feeling. Forgiveness rights the wrong.

4. *I am ...* relates to personal self, desires, dreams, self-esteem and the like.

5. *Gratitude* is all about remembering to count your blessings and say thank you.

6. *Our thoughts and words* gives revelations regarding thought energies, and makes you realise how powerful that energy is. It can make or break a person.

7. *Healing prayers* is to do with healing. The more we ask for a healing, the more healing energy is created. Suddenly the door opens to opportunities for the

Stefka Harp

person to find healing. It certainly helped me; this is how I know it works.

8. *Peace and harmony.*

If you have read all of the poetry books from 1–7 numerous times, cleared the clutter of unwanted memories, nullified the negative energies created over time, sent other people's energy back where it belongs, you will be feeling a burden-free spirit.

This burden-free spirit will have progressed so far spiritually that when the *Peace and harmony* poems are read, there will be feelings of peace, calm, serenity and oneness with the world and the universe. This oneness gives a feeling of wholeness within. Presto! A spiritual enlightenment, one with the Almighty; it is a nourishment for the Holy Spirit within. I wouldn't like to feel any less than the tranquillity around me. I cannot see the energy around me that I created, but I certainly can feel it.

A habit has been created of being a positive thinker, showing kindness, and releasing loving thoughts to the Divine self and the world. Have in mind that we are all Divine creations, miraculously complex and diverse. Please spare a thought for others and be more accepting of their diversity, be it in looks, faith or ideas.

Enjoy reading, and have a happy and prosperous life!

Stefka Harp

Peace & harmony

Perpetual love Divine, around me eternally,
Essential it is to give it freely.
Adamant I am to do it cheerfully,
Calm and serene, to be in harmony,
Endless peace bountifully.

Stefka Harp

Submit to loving thoughts I do,
Embrace the Sublime too.
Remarkably I go through,
Energy Divine to woo. I
Nurture body and soul,
Inner peace to uphold,
Transforming into a Divine child, in truth,
Yielding serenity within to soothe.

Peace & harmony

Dynamic my loving thoughts are,
Invisible and bizarre,
Vast they are and go afar
Impossible to know if they are on par,
Nevertheless I feel the energy wrap around
Effortlessly, I have been divinely crowned.

Laughing all the way
Ocean of love to convey,
Vitality without delay
Essential for me to thrive every day.

Stefka Harp

Lean on the Divine, I always do,
Occasion to celebrate too,
Vibrancy to me and you,
Everlasting love comes through.

Pouring blessings, for
Earthly peace infinitely,
Angelic feelings ultimately,
Calmness immediately,
Energy Divine, illuminating definitely.

As long as I live and beyond,
Now and forever troubles gone,
Delightfully, life prolonged.

Peace & harmony

Healthy, wealthy and stress free
Attainment for all is my plea,
Radiant I am and free, from
Morn and beyond I do my chores cheerfully,
Overjoyed I am and tread carefully,
Nutty as I might be, but I agree
Embracing all of the above is the key, for
Yielding Love, Peace and Harmony.

Tenacity I have shown
Over the years I have grown,

Be it in body and mind or Soul Divine
Ever so to be gentle and kind.

Holy Spirit within,
On the go and away from sin
Lively and keen,
Young and vibrant as I have always been.

It is what it is, no doubt
Soul Divine is all about.

Timeless universe flows,
Heavenly peace grows
Eternally, Soul Divine glows.

Keep faith, and tell the truth cheerfully
Equally, universal love give freely, and
Yes, when you speak truth, you are in harmony. Be

Fair, a just and kind soul,
Overall, love Divine will unfold a
Road leading to a pot of gold.

Peace & harmony

Peace-loving child I am and obey
Effort well worth while, I say.
Another enjoyable day on the way,
Captivating the colours of the ray,
Elevation of the soul here to stay.

As always I appreciate the moment I am in,
None other counts more within.
Delightful my life is and has been.

Heavenly, I hold dear and aspire,
All my loving thoughts to be on fire,
Rare but true, everyone is my friend,
Mind you, some of them I haven't met yet,
Other than that, there is no hate,
Not now, not ever and no regret,
Yielding peace and harmony like a magnet.

Merciful the Divine is, I declare.
Yes, the Almighty does care.

Humble nature in me grows,
Ample love outpours.
Rejuvenation soars,
Motivation bestows.
Overflow of happiness to know,
Never mind what was before.
Incredible expectations without limit,
Offsetting illumination like a magnet,
Union with the holy is ultimate,
Solemn promise I vow, indefinite.

Thus, my vision is glorious life ahead of me,
Humble and burden free.
Overwhelmed with joy and harmony,
Unfolding every moment as they should be.
Genuine humility is the key.
Here and now, heart and soul
Trust to uphold,
Serenity to unfold,

Peace & harmony

Always within my domain,
Raising my conciseness to maintain
Endless spiritual sustenance to be humane.

Pray I do and believe, by
Unleashing harmonious thoughts to receive
Remarkable supremacy day and night,
Everlasting peace to my delight.

Hereby utmost purity,
Expecting innermost harmony,
Always attaining,
Restoring and gaining
Thy kindness, eternally maintaining.

Stefka Harp

Merriment I find, when I
Yearn to do good deeds and be kind.

Gracefully I do it most of the time,
Overall I am humble and can verify,
Only way to align is by
Dedication to the Divine.

Devotion I have for the Serene Highness,
Endless purification and holiness
Encouragement in you and me, I
Dare stand out with glee,
Saintly, good deeds to do and be in harmony.

Peace & harmony

Amplifying my good deeds,
Round they come to meet my needs
Ever-powerful positive energy exceeds.

Merit of mine
Yearning to be Divine.

Non-stop to forgive,
Eternal love Divine to give,
Endless loving thought energy until
Destiny fulfilled and
Serenity achieved.

Off I go
Non-stop to explore,

Temptation of evil to overthrow
Hence holiness to flow,
Embrace it I do, on the count of four.

Determined I am, whatever I do,
It's important to be true,
Verity to myself I coo,
Invigorating Soul Divine to pursue.
Night and day I do it affectionately
Evidently, I trust the spirit within indefinitely.

In no time, inner peace upon my soul.

Calmly, troubles and wrongs long gone,
Ample happiness by dawn,
Now and forever I divinely carry on.

Confidently I proceed with passion
Opening a window for compassion,
Unfolding good virtues and I am gladdened
Neither more nor less, but strengthened,
Triumphantly driven and fortune given.

Peace & harmony

Faithfully I am treading the path of my destiny
Obediently, even though destiny is a mystery,
Ready and willing, I do it fervently.

Empowered I am by the Serene Highness, my
Thoughts are Divine likeness,
Expecting Thy holiness to
Reign supreme, willingness
Near and far as always.
Attention I pay to my wellness,
Living a life of righteousness.

Paramount it is to be living
Every moment in spirit,
Afresh as a newborn, I shine
Cheer and chime, it's not a crime.
Endless love Divine, I find

Thy guidance fervently, and
Oneness with the holy heartily.

Fortunate I am peace to find,
Impressed deeply to remind me
Never to resign, nor
Deviate from being Divine.

Stefka Harp

Inner peace brings out the best in me,

At long last I am in harmony.
Merrily I live my life and feel free. The

Amazements ahead of me are real,
Near and far, I spread goodwill.

I inspire to the best of my will,
Mastering the divinity, until I
Acquire holiness to overspill.
God grant the above to everyone who is keen,
Energy Divine to flow and shield.

Peace & harmony

Off I go and submit
For ever to be a kind spirit.

To me and the world
Harmonious days galore,
Essential for holiness to uphold.

Holiness is to take part,
Only way to start by
Loving thoughts to impart,
Yesterday, today and beyond, I do it with all my heart.

Destined I am to be holy
Entirely, and that's my story,
Vehemently I glory.
Only one thing on my mind,
Time for body and soul to be unified,
Inner most spirit glorified.
Only way to be free,
Now and forever in harmony.

Turning point in my life,
Order of the day is to be Divine.

Peace & harmony

Tranquillity is coming to be,
Humility bestowed upon me,
Expecting nothing but blooming days to see.

Happiness will bring an
Overflow of trust within, for
Love Divine to pursue and woo,
Youthfulness and holiness too.

By gone is the meltdown,
Lost I was and rundown, I am
Eager the above to renounce,
Saintly peace I have found,
Sacred heart has been crowned.
Excitement at best,
Definitely I am blessed.

Impression of the above I caress,

Affection flowing, I confess,
Manifesting nothing but success.

Sheer joy to reach the summit,
An infinite spiritual attainment.
Loving the spirit within,
Victory definite and
Always on target.
True illumination in life,
Indicating I am alive.
Oneness with the Divine,
Nifty way for holiness to find.

Peace & harmony

The ultimate outcome is awesome, when
One gains wisdom.

Fair it is to say and convey,
Invigoration of the soul and being brave,
Necessary for you and me to pray,
Divine order to obey and have a good day.

Stefka Harp

Sheer pleasure to know peace,
Elation of the soul to increase.
Ready to explore,
Eager to soar.
Nobly to inspire
In quest of holiness I aspire.
These loving thoughts do soothe,
Yielding peace and good mood.

In so far as I submit herein,
Namely to the spirit within.

Alliance with the Almighty too,
Lovingly I go through
Luminous energy I pursue.

Peace & harmony

I shall make it clear,
Truth within will domineer
Sufficiently for the Almighty to appear.

Majestic sight to my delight
Igniting holiness in its might,
Gratitude to you, Almighty, you are dynamite.
Heavenly serenity pervading everything,
Thus always bringing harmony.

Stefka Harp

Pure light within,
Along with patience herein,
Together, peace they bring.
Inclined to make you sing,
Ever so like a zing,
Noble and glorious like a king,
Catching the essence of the free will
Eternally to the extreme.

Calmness and serenity upon me,
Resist evil I do fervently.
Expecting holiness cheerfully,
Ample wealth willingly.
Trust the Divine I do clearly.
Everlasting peace within I feel
Sufficient for body, mind and soul to heal.

Peace & harmony

Perfect way to start the day,
Excellent events underway.
Almighty, I obey.
Come what may, I do not stray,
Enjoying the peace found on the way.

Wisdom reigns supreme,
Intuition like a sunbeam,
Tranquillity as well, oh, what a dream!
Here and now bestows self-esteem,
Invigorating body and brain
Night and day within my domain.

Stefka Harp

I have a goal to

   Capture peace on the whole, to be
   Happy and unfold my
   Everlasting dynamic soul.
   Redemption I have asked for,
   In all fairness, furthermore,
   Soul Divine to be
   Heavenly kind and free.

   Tender loving care and easy flow.
   Honour and grace for sure,
   Eternal holiness and harmony in my core.

Peace & harmony

Patience within always,
Everyday with willingness.
Among all the life's ups and downs, I
Cherish the Divine crowns that
Encourage me not to have meltdowns.

Who do I turn to? But the
Infinite, Almighty you,
Time and again without argue.
Happily I go through.
It's true!
Nothing, but love, trust and respect I pursue.

Beautiful day, hot sun in the sky,
Life goes on, even if we fry.
Enough to make us cry.
Seek the Divine all the time
Silently repent, it's not a crime.
In no time blessings from the Divine,
Now and forever, for being generous and kind.
Grasp the wisdom within to find
Serenity and peace with time.

First of all, send out a blessing prayer
Over and over, and prepare to
Release loving energies as often as you could.

Allow universal love to flare, as it should.
Luck is pouring here, there and everywhere
Loving Almighty blesses us all with Divine care.

Peace & harmony

Mellow Almighty, you are,
Yes, here, there and everywhere,

Day in and day out,
Ample joy wrapped around.
Yes, delightful feelings I have found
Sweet and serene without doubt.

On and on, infinitely
Festive time ahead of me definitely.

Joyful days will domineer
Overwhelming peace to cheer.
Yes, priceless harmonious life is here.

Pure thought brings a glow,
Effort worthwhile for sure,
Allows me spiritually to grow.
Calm and peace galore,
Eternally to flow.

Blessed I am, and allowed
Replenishment beyond any doubt,
Immense saturation for my needs,
Non-stop for my good deeds.
God grant the above to everyone,
Soothe body, mind and soul, with plenty of fun.

Life lived in the here and now,
It's mighty awesome, and I vow to
Faithfully follow the Divine light,
Eminently to bring delight

Peace & harmony

To illuminate my way
Outright, each and every day.

Furthermore, I plea that Thy guidance be
Richly provided with abundance,
Unfailingly, for whatever I do.
In no time a breakthrough.
Therefore a vibrant rose garden,
Innocence within, fragrant,
Over and above pleasant,
Nothing less than brilliant.

Stefka Harp

Patience is a virtue clearly, I
Expect to be in harmony.
Always peace and wisdom within,
Core of my life. Holiness to instil,
Eternal soul's elation to thrill.

Wonders like rainbows
Immensely the Divine pours,
Tranquillity flows.
Heavenly peace for me to know
In its entirety, therefore
Night or day, wisdom galore.

Peace & harmony

Blessed and divinely caressed, I feel,
Rejuvenated and divinely healed,
Invigorated and heartwarmingly awesome,
Non-stop my spirit to blossom.
Gentleness wrapped around in delight
Soothing body and soul day and night.

Well and truly here is the clue,
I am an image of Almighty you.
Symbol of true me,
Dignified and free,
Obedience is the key,
Merriment to all and be in harmony.

Stefka Harp

I have a genie whose magic I pursue.

Wishing is easy, when you know how to.
In no time, wishes come true. I
Sing and praise Almighty you,
Harmonious loving energy I woo.

Anything is possible with the Divine, I
Never underestimate the power of the sublime,
Dynamic and pure like an innocent child.

Peace & harmony

Complacency is not something to dwell on,
Only loving thoughts to swell,
Merrily I go with life and forgive,
Marvellous way to live.
Another day to give and receive
Nothing but loving energies with all my heart.
Divinity and prosperity at my command.

Stefka Harp

Hopefully, my day dreams grew.
Amazingly, they came true,
Richly provided and blessed too. I
Marvel the blessing with zest,
Obstacles removed, and celebrate
Nifty way for success.
Yes, all peace and harmony to manifest.

Peace & harmony

Beam with joy I do and pray
Endless peace and harmony night and day,
Shaping destiny every day.
Therefore, my message to convey,
Only truth and justice will prevail.
Wisdom every day,
Epic journey without delay,
Divinity is the game I play.

Illusory I might be!

And not easy to see, it is clear, but
Mighty I am as ever, and sincere.

Hence, I am here whenever the need,
Essential for you to know indeed,
Ray of hope a gift for you.
Embrace it through and through.

Nurture love in earnest,
Only love and trust
Withstand the evil around us.

Thoughts of love make you Divine,
Harmoniously with time,
Everlasting, glorious peace you'll find.

Peace & harmony

As always, spiritual attainment is a must,
Luminous energy approaching fast,
My love for you day and night
Is infinite and dynamite.
Glory upon it in delight.
Honours as well to revere
To eternity to endear,
Youthfulness forever to domineer.

Winsome Divine creations I praise,
Health and happiness ablaze,
Immense wealth to amaze,
Swiftly to manifest without delays.
Pristine love for you I embrace,
Elation and loving thought energies to gain,
Revealing amazing light Divine within your domain,
Eternally for body and brain,
Day in and day out peace and harmony to reign.

Young and joyful I have been,
Only youthfulness within my
Unfolding kind and generous spirit.
None other but the Divine,
Graciously will guide vibrancy for me to find.

An accomplishment all the more,
Never to regress but restore,
Delicate Soul Divine to glow.

Vitality, once established,
Infinitely ills banished,
Brilliant good health lavished.
Radiance from a star,
Alight and bizarre,
Non-stop shines near and far.
Tremendously overjoyed we are.

Peace & harmony

Whoever you are, be always keen, it's
Essential to begin

Alliance with the Serene Highness.
Rejuvenation and kindness,
Everlasting holiness.

Destined to be holy, for
Inner peace and harmony.
Vibrant as always I have been,
Invigorated body and mind ready to spring
Non-stop to give universal love, and live
Each and every day to be serene and forgive.

By gone are the days of troubles outright, now I
Look to the Divine light,
Enables me to make it right,
Seeking holiness in delight.
Satisfaction for heart and soul,
Innocence and purity on the whole,
None other but the Holy Spirit will ignite
Generosity and kindness in its all might.
Spellbound blessings by candlelight.

Peace & harmony

Blessed and healthy are my body and soul,
Obedience on the whole,
Dignity to uphold,
Young and vibrant, never old.

Accomplishment within my domain is
Necessary to maintain, a
Desire to be humane.

Saintly deeds in my name, as
Often as I can without complaint,
Up and away to attain
Life immortal for body and brain.

Stefka Harp

Gratitude to the Divine forever,
Lifelong commitment to flare.
Overflow of possibilities to yield,
Rejuvenation for body to heal,
Incredible transformation will begin.
First and foremost spirit to thrill,
Inner most goodwill to fulfil,
Eager to reveal
Devotion, truth and Divine shield.

Peace & harmony

Haven I have found,
Apparently I have been crowned,
Redemption in my name,
Magical feelings within my domain.
Overwhelming holiness is upon me,
Next, all troubles long gone
In no time, healthy and wealthy by dawn.
Off I go and caress my soul,
Unburdened and peaceful, I carry on,
Sublime serenity I thus bring on.

Invigoration and elation everywhere,

Astonishing harmony, I declare.
Mighty Divine wisdom always does flare.

Stefka Harp

A society with no arts is like a barren land,
Rare beauty is art, something that pleases the brain.
To deny arts would be unkind, a
Syndrome that equals a crime.

Intellect without expression of art, is
Nothing more than soul without a heart.

Peace & harmony

Sure, you would agree art brings harmony,
Over and above being humane,
Calmness and joy within our domain.
Insisting on more art is a must,
Embrace the priceless talent fast.
Trust and respect creates connection,
Yes, why then obstacles and rejection?

Stefka Harp

Selection of thoughts I behold,
Eerie it might sound, but I've been told,
Redemption overall, no
Excuse, and loving thoughts with heart and soul.
Nobly I send them out to
Illuminate the crowd.
Thy Kingdom to seek,
Yearning for truth to know and speak.

Peace & harmony

Willingly, from heart and soul, an outpour.
In no time, forgiveness galore,
Tender loving care to the core.
Hallelujah, ocean of love to roar an
Invisible powerful melody, and more,
Non-stop propels serenity to soar.

Stefka Harp

Generous and kind,
Always on time,
Image of the holy
Lively and jolly.

Caring to the core,
Attention to detail galore.
Remarkable you are,
Therefore you'll go far.
Well and truly you are a star,
Reliable and always above par.
Incredible honesty, I agree,
Gracious with no boundary,
Heart and soul in harmony,
Talent you display clearly.

Peace & harmony

Eager to do it right,
Devotion to your work downright
Inner most sincerity, I impart
Timeless gratitude with all my heart.
Overflow of well wishes to you in delight,
Ray of hope, health and happiness as well outright.

Humbly, I feel at peace,
Any time, harmonious thoughts I release.
Round the clock, with all my heart,
Miraculously those awesome energies come,
Opportunity for creating a habit,
Nourishment for the brain to inhabit,
Yes, peace and harmony for ever established.

About the author

Stefka was born during World War II in a small village tucked away in the foothills of a big mountain in Eastern Macedonia.

Her family, like others in the village, gained their food from the land. It was a self-sufficient household. This lifestyle built much confidence in her and her siblings.

She migrated to Australia in 1972, where she still resides. She finished her degree, and a diploma in counselling, and gained jobs in the welfare sector.

The last seven years before she retired were spent supporting those who experienced domestic violence. While working with people, she used her knowledge of the power of thought as a creator of our destiny. She has seen astonishing improvements when people change their attitude and implement positive and loving thoughts. Prayer, forgiveness, hope and faith go hand in hand with positive growth and attitudes.

Academic achievements

Diploma of Community Services Management

Southbank Institute of TAFE 2006

Diploma in Counselling

Australian Institute of Counsellors 1993–1994

Bachelor of Arts Degree (Major Psychology)

University of Queensland 1989

Economics, book keeping & accounting

Business Studies College (Macedonia)

www.ingramcontent.com/pod-product-compliance
Lightning Source LLC
Chambersburg PA
CBHW061254040426
42444CB00010B/2382